CONTENTS

Nutritional Guidelines per Serving — 5
The Negroni Forerunners — 7
Americano — 8
Milano Torino — 10
Recipe Variations — 11
Punt e Mes Chocolate Negroni — 12
Count Mast Negroni — 14
Unusual Negroni — 16
Italian Gentleman — 17
Expert Level Negroni — 18
Clarified Negroni — 20
Quill Cocktail — 22
Negroni Fizz — 24
Truffle Dark Chocolate Negroni — 26
Pomegranate Negroni — 28
Rosemary Mezcal Negroni — 30
Negroni with Prosecco Foam — 32
Chocolate Negroni — 34
Bulevar — 36
All English Negroni — 37
Oaxacan Negroni — 39

Aperol Negroni	41
Negroni Swizzle	42
Negroni Gin Flip	44
Agavoni	46
Negroni Ice Cream Float	48
Sbagliato	50
The Professional	52
Cold Brew Negroni	54
What Food Does It Go Well With	55
FAQs	60
Conclusion	62

The Negroni is a stronger version of the Americano, a cocktail made of club soda, Campari, and sweet vermouth. Count Camilo Negroni loved his Americano yet he was craving for something stronger. Sometime in 1919, he instructed his bartender to create something that is like the Americano but with a kick. Since the club soda was the weak link for this cocktail, it was replaced with gin and so the Negroni was born.

The cocktail made a huge breakthrough that year that the Negroni family started their distillery that same year. They also started bottling Negroni and sold it under the name Negroni Antico. Since then, the Negroni has been a staple in any bar scene.

NUTRITIONAL GUIDELINES PER SERVING

Calories   200

Calories from fat   0   1 %DV*

Sodium   3.5 mg   0 %DV

Carbohydrates   12 g   4 %DV

Fiber   0 g   0 %DV

Sugar   10 g   12 %DV

Protein   0.1 g

1 serving = 3 ounces

*Note: Percent Daily Values are based in a 2000-calorie diet

Tools Required To Make The Drink

- Rocks glass - best bar glass to use in serving the Moscow Mule
- Jigger - a bar tool used to measure the ingredients for cocktails
- Bar spoon - a long-stemmed, usually twisted spoon used for stirring cocktails

Ingredients

- 1 oz gin
- 1 oz Campari
- 1 oz sweet vermouth

Steps To Make

1. Pour all the ingredients over ice into a rocks glass.
2. Stir and squeeze an orange peel over the glass.
3. Drop the orange peel into the glass and serve.

THE NEGRONI FORERUNNERS

The Negroni is the ultimate result of constant tweaking of cocktails prior to its creation. Here, we pay homage to the cocktails that gave us this amazing aperitif.

AMERICANO

The Americano is the nearest relative of the Negroni as this is the cocktail that inspired Count Camillo Negroni to make it into a stronger Negroni by exchanging the club soda with gin. It tempers the bitterness of the Campari by adding club soda.

Ingredients:

- 1 ½ oz Campari
- 1 ½ oz sweet vermouth
- Soda water

Steps to make

1. In a highball glass, add some ice.
2. Pour in the Campari and sweet vermouth. Stir.
3. Top with soda water.

4. Garnish with a lemon peel.

MILANO TORINO

The Milano Torino is the grandfather of the Negroni, usually made with equal parts Campari and vermouth. It derives its name from the place where Campari is made (Milan) and Turin where the vermouth was made. It was first created in the 1860s.

Ingredients

- 30ml Campari
- 30ml Vermouth di Torino

Steps to make

1. Combine both ingredients into a double old fashioned glass.
2. Add ice and stir briefly.
3. Garnish with an orange slice.

RECIPE VARIATIONS

The Negroni has so many variations that will possibly fill a short book. Let's take a look at some of them.

PUNT E MES CHOCOLATE NEGRONI

Punt e Mes is a good way to describe the vermouth's flavor bittersweet profile - 1 point sweet and half-point bitter. It is a good companion for the Campari but makes it a less vivid red with its brown color. Perfect for the Chocolate Negroni.

Ingredients

- 1 oz gin
- ¾ oz Punt e Mes Italian vermouth
- ¾ oz Campari
- ¼ oz Bols Creme de Cacao White

- 2-3 dashes of Chocolate Bitters

Steps to make

1. Combine all the ingredients into your double old fashioned glass.
2. Stir with ice for 20-30 seconds.
3. Garnish with an orange wedge.

COUNT MAST NEGRONI

Count Mast Negroni swaps the Campari with Jagermeister, a digestif made of 56 herbs and spices giving it an extra sweetness and body.

Ingredients

- 1 oz Jagermeister
- 1 oz Sweet Vermouth
- 1 oz gin

Steps to make

1. Combine all the ingredients into your double old fashioned glass.

2. Stir with ice for 20-30 seconds.
3. Garnish with a lemon twist.

UNUSUAL NEGRONI

Tired of the bitter Negroni? Try the less assertive version of the cocktail in the Unusual Negroni.

Ingredients

- 1 ¼ oz gin
- 1 oz Aperol
- 1 oz Lillet Blanc

Steps to make

1. Combine all the ingredients into your double old fashioned glass.
2. Stir with ice for 20-30 seconds.
3. Garnish with a slice of grapefruit.

ITALIAN GENTLEMAN

A good riff for the Negroni which swaps bourbon for the gin and without the sweet vermouth. This is the more manly version of the Negroni.

Ingredients

- 1 ½ oz Campari
- 1 ½ oz bourbon
- ¾ oz fresh lemon juice
- ¼ oz rich syrup (2:1 sugar-water)
- 2 dashes orange bitters

Steps to make

1. Add all the ingredients to your cocktail shaker
2. Shake & double strain into a chilled coupe glass
3. Garnish with a twist of lemon

EXPERT LEVEL NEGRONI

Take your Negroni to the next level by serving it in a smoky ice sphere instead of directly into the rocks glass.

Ingredients

- ½ oz gin
- ½ oz Campari
- ½ oz sweet vermouth
- Cherry wood chips

Tools

- Cocktail smoker
- Ice sphere mold
- Soldering iron
- Food syringe

Steps to make

1. Make the ice sphere.
    1. Fill your ice sphere mold with water.
    2. Cover the top hole with your finger then turn it over.
    3. If there are bubbles in it, add more water to remove the bubbles.
    4. Freeze it for 11 hour and 30 minutes. Turn the mold over and freeze for another 1 hour and 30 minutes.
    5. Heat up a clean soldering iron.
    6. Gently touch the tip of the iron to the top of the sphere.
    7. Remove the water in the sphere using a food syringe.
    8. When all the water is removed, return the ice sphere into the freezer to harden it further. Use a plastic bowl to hold it.
2. Make the cocktail.
    1. Fill mixing glass with ice cubes to chill it.
    2. Stir for 30 seconds. Pour out the water.
    3. Add the gin, Campari, and sweet vermouth. Set aside.
    4. In a rocks glass, add a large cube of ice with a hole drilled into it. Use the soldering iron.
    5. Add smoke into the hole in the ice by adding the cherry wood chips into the cocktail smoker and directing the hose to the hole.
    6. Position an ice sphere on top of the smoked ice.
    7. Pour the cocktail into the hole on the ice sphere.

CLARIFIED NEGRONI

Red is a bit aggressive? Clarify it with milk.

Ingredients

For the cocktail

- 1 oz Empress 1908 gin
- 2 oz clarified bitter liqueur*
- Grapefruit wedge

For the clarified liqueur

- 4 oz Aperol
- 4 oz Cocchi di Torino
- 3 oz Vodka
- 1 oz Regan's orange bitters
- 1/2 oz wormwood tincture

- 1/2 tbsp fresh grated ginger
- 3 oz grapefruit juice
- 3 oz whole milk

Steps to make

1. Make the clarified liqueur
    1. Mix everything except the milk together.
    2. Then pour that mix over the 3 oz of milk.
    3. Stir gently and filter through a coffee filter. If the first drops are cloudy, pour them back over.
2. Make the cocktail
    1. In a mixing glass, add the Empress gin and clarified bitter liqueur.
    2. Add ice and stir for 30 seconds.
    3. Garnish with burnt grapefruit wedge. To burn the grapefruit wedge, scorch it with a bar torch until the rind is blackened and the flesh starts to release the aroma.

QUILL COCKTAIL

Give your classic Negroni a delightful twist by rinsing your serving glass with absinthe, lending it an anise and herbal aroma.

Ingredients

- 1 ½ oz Mythic Gin
- 1 oz Campari
- 1 oz Carpano Antica Sweet Vermouth
- ¼ oz Absinthe

Steps to make

1. In a mixing glass, add the gin, Campari and sweet vermouth.
2. Add ice and stir for 30 seconds.
3. Rinse a coupe glass with absinthe by swirling it for a few

seconds. Pour out the absinthe.
4. Pour the cocktail into the coupe glass and serve.

NEGRONI FIZZ

Created by Ryan Williams, this cocktail is a fusion of the classic Negroni and the Ramos Gin Fizz. Brace yourself with all the shaking, folks, this might be the treat you'll need after that workout!

Ingredients

- 1 ¼ oz gin
- 1 oz sweet vermouth
- ¾ oz Campari
- 2 oz heavy cream powder prepared as to instruction
- ¾ oz simple syrup
- ¼ oz fresh lemon juice
- 1 egg white (or ¾ oz liquid egg white)
- 3 dashes Bittercube Bolivar bitters

- 1 dash orange bitters
- 2 oz chilled club soda
- 3 drops orange blossom water

Steps to make

1. Add the ingredients, except the club soda and orange blossom water into the cocktail shaker.
2. Add 1 ice cube and shake until it melts.
3. Add 2 oz club soda into the serving glass.
4. Add more ice to the shaker to complete the shake.
5. Double strain the cocktail into the club soda.
6. Add the remaining club soda (fill to the brim).
7. Add 3 drops of orange blossom water.
8. Garnish with an orange peel.

TRUFFLE DARK CHOCOLATE NEGRONI

Ready to throw in some serious stuff into your favorite Negroni? If chocolate truffles are delicious as food, it sure is delicious on drinks, despite that signature funky smell. You need at least 24 hours to prepare this delicious digestif if you want to serve it for your next

Ingredients

- 300ml gin
- 250ml sweet vermouth
- 250ml bitter liqueur
- 100g cocoa nibs
- 25g freshly grated truffles
- Slice of truffle for garnish

Steps to make

1. In a large, airtight jar, pour in the gin, sweet vermouth, and bitter liqueur.
2. Drop in the cocoa nibs and truffles then mix well.
3. Cover and let infuse for at least 24 hours.
4. Strain with a cheesecloth into a bottle.

POMEGRANATE NEGRONI

Add a touch of mystique to your Negroni by adding fresh pomegranate arils for that healthy touch.

Ingredients

- 1 oz gin
- 1 oz Campari
- 1 oz sweet vermouth
- ½ pomegranate
- Orange wheel for garnish

Steps to make

1. Mix the gin, Campari, and sweet vermouth in a mixing glass.
2. Add ice and stir to chill.
3. Remove the arils from the half of the pomegranate and drop it into the coupe glass.

4. Pour in your Negroni mix and drop in some ice cubes.
5. Garnish with an orange wheel.

ROSEMARY MEZCAL NEGRONI

Prepare your rosemary-infused mezcal at least 24 hours before you serve this cocktail, giving it a Mexican feel. The rosemary lends a pungent lemony flavor and aroma to the mezcal.

Ingredients

For the rosemary-infused Campari

- 12 oz Campari
- 4 sprigs rosemary sprigs

For the cocktail

- 1 ¼ oz mezcal
- 1 oz sweet vermouth
- 1 oz rosemary-infused Campari
- Garnish: Grapefruit peel; Rosemary sprig

Steps to make

1. Make the rosemary-infused Campari
   1. In a large Mason jar, combine 12 oz Campari and 4 rosemary sprigs and seal.
   2. Let sit at room temperature for 24 hours, shaking occasionally.
   3. Strain out solids and keep in the refrigerator for up to one month.
2. Assemble the cocktail.
   1. Add all ingredients in a mixing glass with ice and stir.
   2. Strain into a rocks glass over fresh ice.
   3. Express oil from a grapefruit peel over the drink and discard.
   4. Using a kitchen torch, flame the rosemary until it smokes and extinguish before serving.

NEGRONI WITH PROSECCO FOAM

Give yourself a treat with this creamy and frothy Negroni recipe. This recipe makes five 3-oz servings.

Ingredients

For the prosecco foam

- 2 cups orange juice, divided
- Orange zest from 1 orange
- 1 tbsp fructose powder
- 1 tbsp pectin
- 2 egg whites
- 3 oz prosecco

For the cocktail

- ½ cup gin

- ½ cup Campari
- ½ cup sweet vermouth
- ⅓ cup soda water

Steps to make

1. Make the prosecco foam.
    1. In a saucepan, heat up 1 cup orange juice and the zest from 1 orange over low heat.
    2. Mix the fructose and pectin until pectin is dissolved.
    3. Add the fructose-pectin mixture to the saucepan.
    4. Mix for a while then remove from heat. Let cool for 30 minutes.
    5. Add the remaining 1 cup orange juice, egg whites, and prosecco.
    6. Beat with an immersion blender for 10 seconds.
    7. Strain and transfer to a siphon bottle and chill in the freezer.
2. Assemble the cocktail.
    1. Fill a serving glass with ice.
    2. Add 3 oz of the Negroni mix.
    3. Top with the Prosecco foam.

CHOCOLATE NEGRONI

Take decadence to a new level with this chocolate Negroni garnished with chocolate orange.

Ingredients

- 1 ½ oz. gin
- 1 ½ oz. Gran Classico Bitter Liqueur
- 1 ½ oz. Sweet Red Vermouth
- ½ oz. Creme de Cacao
- 3 dashes Chocolate Bitters
- Chocolate Orange as garnish

Steps to make

1. Combine gin, Gran Classico, sweet red vermouth, créme de cacao, and chocolate bitters in a mixing glass with ice and stir.

2. Strain mix into a rocks glass over ice and garnish with a chocolate orange.

BULEVAR

Gotta love this spicy riff of the Negroni with the addition of the Ancho Reyes Chile Liqueur made with dried and smoky poblano (also called ancho) chiles.

Ingredients

- ¾ oz sweet vermouth
- ½ oz Campari
- ½ oz Ancho Reyes Chile Liqueur
- 1 ½ oz bourbon

Steps to make

1. Mix everything together.
2. Add ice and stir for 30 seconds.
3. Strain over new ice cubes in a rocks glass.
4. Garnish with a cherry.

ALL ENGLISH NEGRONI

Try your Negroni with all English ingredients. Blackdown gin and vermouth is made in Blackdown, Sussex while Stellacello is made in London. The Stellacello is the slightly sweeter version of the Campari.

Ingredients

- 1 oz Sussex dry gin
- 1 oz Silver Birch vermouth
- 1 oz Stellacello grapefruit liqueur
- Dehydrated orange for garnish

Steps to make

1. Fill rocks glass halfway with ice.
2. Pour the gin, vermouth, and Stellacello into the rocks glass.

3. Stir for 30 seconds to chill well.
4. Garnish with a dehydrated orange slice.

OAXACAN NEGRONI

Indulge in some smoky take of the classic Negroni, minus the sweet vermouth. The mezcal gives it a hint of smokiness while the Cocchi Americano gives it a sweetness that balances the bitter Campari.

Ingredients

- ¾ oz silver tequila
- ¼ oz mezcal
- 1 oz Cocchi Americano
- 1 oz Campari

Steps to make

1. Add all ingredients into a mixing glass.
2. Add lots of ice and stir for 30 seconds.

3. Strain into a serving glass. May be served with ice.
4. Squeeze an orange peel over the glass and drop the peel in.

APEROL NEGRONI

Aperol is tamer in terms of bitterness compared to

Ingredients

- 1 oz gin
- 1 oz sweet vermouth
- 1 oz Aperol
- Lemon wheel for garnish

Steps to make

1. Mix all ingredients in a glass.
2. Add ice and stir vigorously until chilled.
3. Garnish with a lemon wheel.

NEGRONI SWIZZLE

Hot summer day? Cool off with your favorite Negroni with a riff. Lots of ice and soda for that super cool, slightly fizzy cocktail.

Ingredients

- 1 oz gin
- 1 oz Campari
- 1 oz sweet vermouth
- 1 oz soda water

Steps to make

1. Fill a highball glass with crushed ice.
2. Add gin, Campari, and sweet vermouth.
3. Swizzle with a bar spoon until your glass frosts up.

4. Add the soda water.
5. Garnish with a piece of orange or twist.

NEGRONI GIN FLIP

Ingredients

- Egg
- 1 oz Gin
- 1 oz Campari
- 1 oz Sweet Vermouth
- ¼ oz rich sugar syrup

Steps to make

1. Dry shake a whole egg for 15 seconds. Dry shaking is shaking the egg without the ice. It produces more froth.

2. Add the remaining ingredients
3. Shake & strain into an double old fashioned glass
4. Garnish with a twist of orange.

AGAVONI

A good word play for the agave from which the tequila is made and the Negroni gives you the Agavoni.

Ingredients

- ¾ oz tequila
- ¾ oz Campari
- ¾ oz sweet vermouth
- 2 dashes of Orange Bitters

Steps to make

1. Add all the ingredients to your mixing glass
2. Stir for approximately 30 seconds.

3. Strain over ice into an double old fashioned glass
4. Garnish with a twist of grapefruit.

NEGRONI ICE CREAM FLOAT

Do not be fooled with the ice cream, it's not what you might expect. Rich, bittersweet cocktail with a kick of slight pepper taste of the juniper berries.

Ingredients

For the juniper ice cream

- 10 juniper berries
- 2 large scoops of vanilla ice cream

For the Negroni syrup

- 1 ½ oz gin
- 1 ½ oz sweet vermouth
- 1 ½ oz Campari
- ¾ cup sugar

For the cocktail

- 1 ½ oz gin
- ½ oz Campari
- 4 oz grapefruit soda

Steps to make

1. Make the juniper ice cream.
    1. Use a mortar and pestle to crush juniper berries.
    2. Add to soft ice cream and mix through.
2. Make the Negroni syrup
    1. Combine ingredients into a saucepan.
    2. Simmer for approx 10 minutes.
    3. Reduce until syrup is thicker and honey-like in texture.
3. Assemble the cocktail
    1. Combine the gin, Campari and grapefruit soda in a highball glass.
    2. Add the juniper ice cream.
    3. Drizzle with the Negroni syrup.
    4. Garnish with more juniper berries.

SBAGLIATO

When one mistake makes the best accomplishment - that's what Sbagliato is. Literally meaning "mistaken", the bartender unknowingly swapped gin with sparkling wine while making a Negroni. This is one mistake that gained a lot of accolades since, at least among bar-goers.

Ingredients

- 1 oz sweet vermouth
- 1 oz Campari
- 1 oz prosecco

Steps to make

1. Mix the sweet vermouth and Campari in a rocks glass.
2. Add ice and stir to chill.
3. Top with the prosecco. Garnish with an orange peel.

THE PROFESSIONAL

You're not a professional drinker unless you can take this overproofed Jamaican rum (126 proof, 63% ABV). This stings more than it should and you're only a professional if you can down this without a wince.

Ingredients

- ½ oz overproofed Jamaican rum
- 1 oz Campari
- 1 ½ oz bourbon

Steps to make

1. Pour the rum, Campari, and bourbon over ice in a rocks glass.
2. Stir to chill.

3. Garnish with a lemon peel.

COLD BREW NEGRONI

Craving for coffee but can't afford to lose sleep? Give in by ordering the Cold Brew Negroni tonight.

Ingredients

- Mr. Black Coffee Liqueur
- 1 oz gin
- 1 oz Campari
- ½ oz Carpano Antica Sweet Vermouth

Steps to make

1. Mix all the ingredients together in a rocks glass.
2. Add ice and stir.

WHAT FOOD DOES IT GO WELL WITH

Campari goes with anything since it is an aperitif. The bittersweet profile of the Negroni is a good way to whet your appetite. Finding good food to pair with Negroni is a fairly easy task.

Bacon Mac & Cheese

Your ultimate comfort food makes a good pairing with Campari. Topped with grated cheese, breadcrumb, and crunchy bacon and baked to gooey perfection. Just what you need to share with friends you're comfortable with.

Zesty Hot Ham and Cheese Crostini

Best served with creamy tomato sauce, this zesty crostini pairs well with the bittersweet Negroni. Better, you can prepare it in 20 minutes. All you need is some baguette and some very basic ingredients you can find in your pantry and fridge.

Bacon Wrapped Dates with Goat Cheese

Glazed with honey-bourbon syrup, this adult version of everyone's favorite bacon wrap is the perfect choice to enjoy with the Negroni. Creamy cheese, salty bacon, and sweet glaze is a truly tasty treat.

Ribeye Steak with Blue Cheese Compound Butter

Who can say no to steak? The Campari is a good aperitif and eating a heavy meal such as this is no problem with your trusty Negroni by your side.

Charcuterie Board

Made with 4 kinds of cheese, crackers and pretzels, cold meats of choice, grapes, nuts of choice, dry fruits of choice and garnished with lettuce and a sprinkle of raisins, this cheese board has everything you need.

FAQS

Why is it called Negroni?

First off, the Negroni is actually a variation of 3 predecessor cocktails - the Americano being its tamer yet closer relative. The Americano was a variation of the Milano-Torino.

It is called Negroni because it was Count Negroni who requested for a stronger alternative to his tame Americano. The bartender, Fosco Scarselli of Casoni Bar in Florence, Italy, the bar that Count Negroni frequented, threw in equal parts of gin, Campari, and sweet vermouth. Since then, it was known as Count Negroni's drink then eventually became known as Negroni.

Who is Count Negroni?

Pascal Olivier Count de Negroni (1829-1913) was a decorated general mostly known for his leading the Battle of Reichshoffen during the Franco-Prussian War of 1870. He retired from the military in 1891 after serving for 44 years. Although many books and articles credit one Camillo Negroni, an Italian Count, as the inventor of the Negroni, the family of Pascal Olivier de Negroni claimed there is no Camillo Negroni. Instead, it was the French Count Negroni who invented the cocktail.

However, evidence showed that there was really an Italian-born Camillo Negroni who was also a count. Books were written on the quest of the real Count Negroni behind the Negroni cocktail. One such book is the The Negroni: Drinking to La Dolce Vita, with Recipes and Lore by Gary Regan. But one fact remains, it was the Italian Negroni family who made the best of the cocktail's fame by starting the Distilleria Negroni in 1919. The distillery is still in operation but no longer owned by the Negroni family.

Can you add soda to a Negroni?

The Negroni is supposed to be a straight, clean drink but many also love using soda or other sources of carbonation to it as you can see in this article.

How is a Negroni served?

Negroni is usually served on the rocks and garnished with an orange swath to differentiate it from Americano, its predecessor which is garnished with a lemon swath.

What is Negroni made of?

Negroni is made of equal parts of gin, sweet vermouth, and Campari and is garnished with an orange swath.

CONCLUSION

Negroni is a good aperitivo. As it is, it is usually drunk before a meal as it serves to whet the appetite. The bittersweet goodness of the cocktail makes it a good choice for an aperitif since it opens the palate well and gets you to eat more. On its own, the classic Negroni has 200 calories for 3-ounce serving and if you opt for frothy versions, it can have more.

Printed in Great Britain
by Amazon